ENGINEERING CHALLENGES

BUILDING TUNNELS

by Samantha S. Bell

FOCUS READERS

WWW.FOCUSREADERS.COM

Focus Readers is distributed by North Star Editions:
sales@northstareditions.com | 888-417-0195

Produced for Focus Readers by Red Line Editorial.

Content Consultant: Joseph F. Labuz, Professor and Department Head, Department of Civil, Environmental, and Geo-Engineering, University of Minnesota

Photographs ©: saoirse2013/Shutterstock Images, cover, 1; javarman3/iStockphoto, 4–5; Simone-/iStockphoto, 7; Mostovyi Sergii Igorevich/Shutterstock Images, 9; Dmitry Kalinovsky/Shutterstock Images, 10–11; gehringj/iStockphoto, 13; VILevi/iStockphoto, 15; verve231/iStockphoto, 17; Gareth Fuller/Press Association/URN:23754797/AP Images, 18–19; AP Images, 21; Kyodo/AP Images, 23; Red Line Editorial, 24–25, 27, 28

ISBN
978-1-63517-258-4 (hardcover)
978-1-63517-323-9 (paperback)
978-1-63517-453-3 (ebook pdf)
978-1-63517-388-8 (hosted ebook)

Library of Congress Control Number: 2017935931

Printed in the United States of America
Mankato, MN
June, 2017

ABOUT THE AUTHOR

Samantha S. Bell is the author of more than 50 nonfiction books for children. She worked for several years for her father, an architect and engineer who created all kinds of structures.

TABLE OF CONTENTS

CHAPTER 1

GOING UNDERGROUND

Anna smiled at her brother in the back seat. Their car was about to travel through the Laerdal Tunnel in Norway. It stretches 15.2 miles (24.5 km). The drive from one side to the other takes more than 20 minutes. Engineers knew such a long drive in a dark tunnel could make people feel **claustrophobic** or tired.

The Laerdal Tunnel links the cities of Laerdal and Aurland in Norway.

For this reason, they designed **caverns** with colored lights. These caverns are every 3.7 miles (6.0 km). They are meant to help people stay alert. Suddenly, Anna's grandfather pulled into a parking bay, and the three got out of the car. They were standing under a mountain!

A tunnel is a long, narrow path under the ground. Tunnels are some of the most challenging projects in engineering and construction. Engineers spend a lot of time planning them. They must determine a route, study the ground, and design the **excavation** method and support. Years may pass between the idea of the tunnel and when construction begins.

The Romans built this tunnel, or cistern, to hold water.

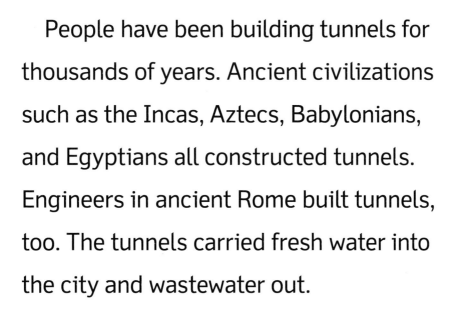

People have been building tunnels for thousands of years. Ancient civilizations such as the Incas, Aztecs, Babylonians, and Egyptians all constructed tunnels. Engineers in ancient Rome built tunnels, too. The tunnels carried fresh water into the city and wastewater out.

For hundreds of years, people built tunnels using simple tools. They used hammers and **chisels** to break through rock. Technology for tunnel building did not change much until the 1600s. That's when workers started blasting away the rock with gunpowder. They later used dynamite.

With the development of trains in the 1800s, engineers began building more tunnels to make travel easier. In the 1950s, tunnel-**boring** machines (TBMs) first were used. These machines could do the job much faster than dynamite.

Today, engineers create tunnels beneath cities, through mountains, and

Tunnels help people move through natural barriers.

even under the ocean. Modern technology has made it possible to build tunnels in places that used to be **impassable**. Tunnels carry water, sewage, power lines, and communication lines. Tunnels also carry people. They are a way to connect cities, states, and even countries.

CHAPTER 2

TUNNEL CONSTRUCTION

Before building a tunnel, engineers spend a lot of time planning. They study the ground to learn how it might act during construction. Engineers also study the site conditions and make sure codes are followed. Codes are safety requirements set by the government.

A worker welds the liner on a subway tunnel.

Engineers then recommend how to build the tunnel. The goal is to build the highest quality tunnel within budget. Engineers decide what support will be needed. They make sure the project is safe for the workers. They also consider how the tunnel will affect other things in that location. For example, tunnels could disrupt wildlife and the natural environment.

In addition, engineers think about the people who will use the tunnel. If the tunnel is a roadway, it must have enough lights for safe travel. Long tunnels also need good **ventilation systems**. These provide fresh air and remove **exhaust**.

Tunnels can have a great effect on their natural surroundings.

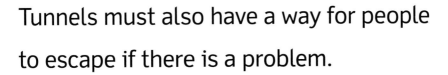

Tunnels must also have a way for people to escape if there is a problem.

All tunnels need to be designed to withstand the weight of the surrounding material. The ground pushes down, and the weight arches around the tunnel.

Depending on the strength of the ground, a support system may be installed. Strong materials help support the tunnel.

Tunnels are constructed in different ways. Soft-ground tunnels are built where the ground is made of soil. If the tunnel is not too deep, workers typically use the cut-and-cover method to build the tunnel. They dig a trench and build the tunnel structure in sections. Then they cover it. Subways, water supply systems, and sewer systems are often associated with soft-ground tunnels.

Rock tunnels are built through mountains or other rocky landforms. They provide faster routes for cars or trains.

Tunnel-boring machines, or TBMs, have rotating cutters that chew through rock.

Workers used to make rock tunnels by blasting the mountains with dynamite. Today, huge TBMs offer another option to chew through the rock.

ENGINEERING DESIGN PROCESS

Engineers use various tools and do many tests in their planning. Once a tunnel is built, they expect the design to be safe and sturdy.

ASK: What will the tunnel be used for? What kind of ground will the tunnel go through? What equipment is needed to build the tunnel? How can the effects on the environment be limited? What safety precautions should be made?

IMAGINE: Brainstorm possible ways to build the tunnel. What excavation method would work best?

PLAN: Draw a diagram of the tunnel. Make a list of materials needed. Write down a list of steps.

CREATE: Follow the plan and build the tunnel.

IMPROVE: What worked with the tunnel? What did not work? Change the design to make the tunnel better. Test it.

TBMs create a tunnel in Thessaloniki, Greece.

Underwater tunnels allow travel under the sea. Some are dug under the ocean floor. Workers often build these tunnels in sections. Then they dig a trench in the sea floor. They float all of the sections into place and sink them. Divers attach the sections together.

CHAPTER 3

THE CHUNNEL

The English Channel separates England and France. In the past, travelers had to cross it by **ferry**. This took 45 minutes. Today a train going through the Chunnel can reach the other side in 20 minutes. The Chunnel is 31 miles (50 km) long. Approximately 23 miles (37 km) are underwater.

A train enters the Chunnel opening in Folkstone, England.

Planners needed to make sure the Chunnel was safe. So they built three tunnels instead of one. A service tunnel runs between two train tunnels. It acts as an escape route in case of a fire. Engineers also created passages every 410 yards (375 m). These allow the trains to switch tracks if necessary.

Construction began in 1988. More than 13,000 people from France and England worked on the Chunnel. They used TBMs to chew through a layer of chalky ground 130 feet (40 m) under the ocean floor. Many of the machines were as long as two football fields. It took three years for the machines to dig all the way through.

Workers on the Chunnel raced to see which side could reach the middle first. The British workers won.

The tunnel was then lined with concrete and cast iron rings.

One year after the Chunnel opened, a fire broke out on a train. Thirty-one people were on the train. They all escaped through the service tunnel. Fires also broke out in 2008 and 2015, but no one was seriously injured.

THE SEIKAN TUNNEL

In 1954, a typhoon sank five ferries on the Tsugaru **Strait** in Japan. More than 1,000 people died. Engineers worked to create a safer crossing. In 1971, construction finally began on the Seikan Tunnel, the world's longest and deepest underwater tunnel.

The ground under the strait was unpredictable. This made the work difficult and slow. Instead of using a TBM, workers had to drill and blast through the earth. They went right through a major fault zone. The tunnel was finished in 1988. More than 14 miles (23 km) of the tunnel's 33 miles (53 km) are under the Tsugaru Strait.

A train enters the Seikan Tunnel in Aomori, Japan.

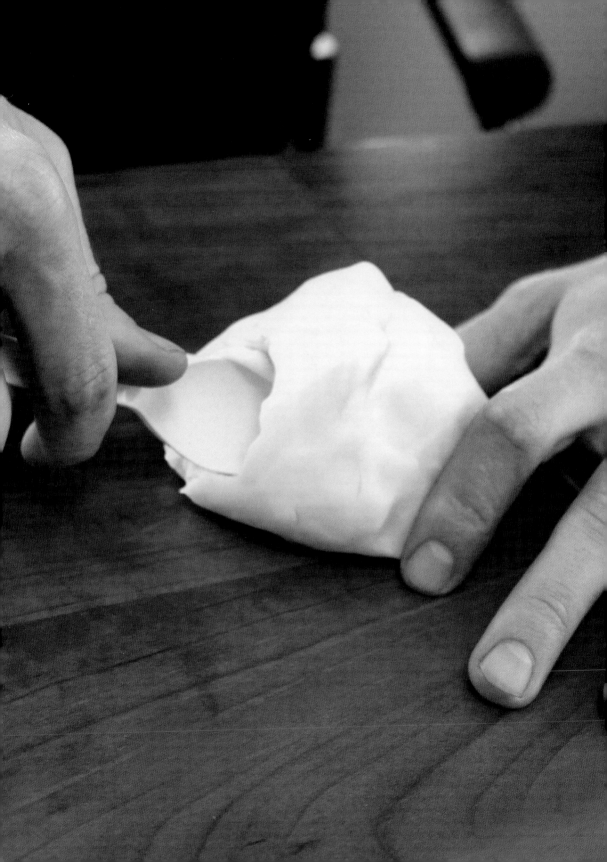

CHAPTER 4

BUILD A TUNNEL

Now it is your turn to build a tunnel through a clay mountain. Can you dig a tunnel through the mountain without it cracking?

Materials:

You will need modeling clay, a spoon, and a toilet paper tube. Also find two or three items with long, thick handles.

You can create a tunnel through modeling clay by simply digging with a spoon.

Procedure:

1. Find a good place to work, such as a table. If needed, you can use a large piece of waxed paper or cardboard to keep your work space clean.

2. Place the modeling clay on the work surface. The clay should be in a big mound, like a mountain.

3. Create a tunnel by digging. Use the spoon to dig a tunnel all the way through the mountain.

4. Next, build a tunnel by boring. Reshape the clay back into a mountain. Then choose an object with a thick, long handle, such as a hairbrush or ladle.

You can bore through the clay by pushing the long handle through it.

5. Place the end of the handle against the side of the mountain. To create the tunnel, push the handle through the clay until it comes out the other side.

A toilet paper roll adds support, which makes the tunnel stronger.

Improve It!

- Your clay mountain might have cracked when you pushed the handle through. How can you change your process to avoid cracking?

- Tunnel-boring machines spin as they cut through rock and clay. What do you think will happen if you rotate the handle as you push it? Try it to find out.

- Linings help support tunnels. How can you use the toilet paper tube to give your tunnel more support?

- Engineers have to choose the right equipment for the job. Try using different objects to bore through the tunnel, such as a marker, a ruler, or even your fingers. Which ones work the best?

FOCUS ON
BUILDING TUNNELS

Write your answers on a separate piece of paper.

1. Write a letter to a friend describing what you learned about the Chunnel.

2. Do you think engineers should continue to design tunnels that take a long time and millions of dollars to build? Why or why not?

3. What technology was introduced to tunnel building during the 1600s?

   A. gunpowder
   B. dynamite
   C. tunnel-boring machines

4. When does the cut-and-cover method work best?

   A. for tunnels in mountainous areas
   B. for tunnels deep in the ground
   C. for tunnels close to the surface

Answer key on page 32.

GLOSSARY

boring
Making a hole by digging away material.

caverns
Large rooms dug out in rock.

chisels
Metal tools that have blades with cutting edges.

claustrophobic
Having a fear of being in narrow or closed-in spaces.

excavation
Digging out earth to create a hole or tunnel.

exhaust
The gas that escapes from an engine.

ferry
A boat used to move people, vehicles, or goods from one place to another.

impassable
Impossible to get across or travel over.

strait
A narrow waterway connecting two large bodies of water.

ventilation systems
A series of connected parts, such as fans, that bring in fresh air and remove stale air.

TO LEARN MORE

BOOKS

Latham, Donna. *Bridges and Tunnels: Investigate Feats of Engineering*. White River Junction, VT: Nomad Press, 2012.

McCue, Camille. *Getting Started with Engineering*. Indianapolis: John Wiley and Sons, 2016.

Sikkens, Crystal. *A Tunnel Runs Through*. New York: Crabtree, 2017.

NOTE TO EDUCATORS

Visit **www.focusreaders.com** to find lesson plans, activities, links, and other resources related to this title.

INDEX

Answer Key: 1. Answers will vary; **2.** Answers will vary; **3.** A; **4.** C